17
Mirrors

Drekkia Writes

Heyy! Thanks for buying a book! Let me Know what you think!

@drekkia

DEDICATION

This book is dedicated to those who have ever suffered in life, won in life or lost in life. I hope you are able to take something from these poems and stories. I hope you feel this, I hope it heals you, and shows you that you are not alone.

Dedicated to ___*Nona Ellis*___
(your name)

TABLE OF POEMS

ACKNOWLEDGMENTS

It is my honor to give thanks to those who have helped me make my first book a reality. I want to thank my mama, Florence Morning above all, for encouraging me to use my gift. I remember her sending me to church to perform my very first spoken word piece that eventually sparked my love for performing. I want to thank my 6th grade teacher Crystal Green for introducing me to poetry, making it fun and helping me to get my first poem published in a book.

I would like to thank my partner Chris James for assisting me, offering creative input, reviewing my content, taking pictures, helping with promotion, and just overall supporting my project with enthusiasm.

I give thanks to my siblings Ronterrio Mayo, Reno Mayo, Tashia Mayo, Maurice Morning and my stepdad Curtis Mayo for all being in my life and always showing me unconditional love.

I would like to thank Foreign Tongues (Chris James, Stacey McAdoo, Ron Mc, Tru, Appollo, Coffy, Osyrus, and Crystal Mercer) your unique styles of writing and performing has had influence on me and I appreciate each and every one of you.

I want to thank my mentor Makeisha Davis for giving me hope and pushing me to my fullest potential when she didn't have to. Special thanks to my mentee Vallejo Lee for my book cover. I literally cried over this process because I went through several design ideas with other people but nothing spoke to my spirit.. I gave Vallejo a photo and color theme and he executed on the first try. Lastly, thank you to Rayshaun Mcnary for the poem art.

I am grateful for everyone who has supported me, inspired me and encouraged me on this journey.

Foreword

By Chris James

I've been reading and hearing these poems written by Drekkia for almost a decade but her words still have a way of traveling through the room and hitting you upside the head when you need it the most, leaving your mouth dropped saying, "DAMN!".

For a while, I recall Drekkia running from her gift of poetry. She'd say poetry ain't what she wanted to do for a living. She would find other hobbies and projects to distract her. But I knew writing and poetry was her gift. Lately, she hasn't gone a day without writing. I watch from across the house or from the driver's seat of the car while we travel and she'll be in a totally different world and I can tell she's moving mountains with her words. When she writes, I can tell she's at peace. I can tell she is whole. So when she writes I just watch, try not to distract her. Often I leave the room because this poem could be the one to change demons to angels, lost souls to found. This poem could be the one to heal the hurt in her heart or the hurt in mine or the hurt in yours.

This book needed to happen. It needed to happen because someone needs to hear her. You need to hear her. Hell, I need to hear her. Her presence alone has pulled me out of so much darkness. Her poems are sure to do the same for you. Her poems are a conversation with every reader. All you got to do is listen. Let the words on each page speak. Let the words resonate. Let the words challenge you. Let them move you to feel and to think. It's okay to feel. It's okay to cry if need be. After all, crying is like taking your soul to the laundry mat. I'm sure a few of us could use a cleansing.

As a matter of fact, take these poems personal. If you're offended, that's good. Sometimes, we need to feel uncomfortable. Nobody in history ever said, "Life is perfect. Let me go change the world." Change is made when we are put in situations of discomfort. I believe art is not meant for just entertainment. It's not meant to make you smile and then you go on being the same as you were. I believe art is meant to inspire action. If the art doesn't do that, in my opinion it hasn't done justice. This book, this body of art will do that. It will inspire action. But you can't come in here being all stubborn like a brick wall because then you may miss what these poems are trying to give you.

Lastly, to my wife, my ONLY FRIEND. I love you. I am so proud of you for trusting whatever higher being or spirit motivated you to give birth to this book. You did it. You made it happen. Now, the world will get a chance to be moved by you and your gift. You are a church and this book will be your bible, so full of holy things. This book will save a young girl who doesn't love herself. This book will teach a woman to not settle for monsters of men. This book will challenge a man to love the woman in his life better than he probably has.

This book will be a best-seller. You are officially an author now. You are breaking all the barriers. First generation college student and graduate, AUTHOR, wife of a fine husband with a beard, big sister and proud aunt, poet, curvy model for major brands. You were voted MOST LIKELY to be famous in HIGH SCHOOL. Now, look at ya. You blowing up girl. You are a big deal for real. I can't even believe I go with you. LOL. Keep being the star you are. Keep loving unconditionally. Keep moving your feet towards everything you want out of this world. Remember, everything you desire is already yours. It's just waiting on you to claim it. Look in your mirror and tell yourself, "God showed out when he made me."

Everyone reading this, after you read this book, please share with a friend and your co-workers. Don't be stingy. Let everybody get this inspiration. Don't keep it to yourself. This book is absolutely the only way WE CAN MAKE AMERICA GREAT AGAIN.

MIRRORED

17 MIRRORS

2 beds

1 bath

4 walls too thin to muffle my cries

My first apartment housed my first experience with

anxiety and depression

A white couch full of impurities.

17 mirrors piercing with my own reflection,

forcing me to face my own truth.

How bad relationships can make you ugly

turn you untrue and unrecognizable to your own-self.

How at 22 years old

I wasn't as perfect as I used to be

How my frame went from medium to extra large,

I was conflicted on how to feel about how weight had

sorted itself throughout my body.

How guilty I felt that God helped me beat the odds

but couldn't quite save my brothers.

How my extreme fear of life made a serial killer out of

me

Too much to digest

So one night,

I tried to scoff down wine, pills and weed

to put me asleep

So that madness

swirling in my body,

would have no one to listen

to the lies it was trying to feed me.

Have you ever felt boxed in and sad

for what appeared to be no reason?

Have you ever wanted to die reluctantly?

Betrayed your body?

Have you ever had someone you love commit treason

against you and convince you it was your fault?

Have you ever been so fucking low

you had to force your lips to smile,

just to convince your own damn self you were happy?

My mirrors

were the only thing that saved me.

Though I saw much pain

I saw how beautiful I was

When I was forcing myself to smile,

I understood that God was going to use me for

something.

So who was I to take my own life?

To disrespect God's labor of love?

What kind of coward would I be,

to let pain get the best of me?

When God gave me the strength of a 1000 lions

How weak would I look to my niece

if I didn't have enough courage

to pick myself and fight

My mirrors gave me LIFE!

Gave me hope

Reminded me I was dope!

That I was powerful

And in control

EMPTY

Condemned to the thought of

not being enough

Feels like being cemented to the torturous idea

that you will never enjoy the peace of

mind you once had before this,

Feels like lack thereof

Like deficient

Feels too little

Real scarce

Like insufficient

Feels like a ½ teaspoon

in a recipe meant for one cup

Feels *unwhole*

Incomplete

Feels like third place

Feels like being half empty

Feels like being a loser

Feels not wanting to be seen

FLAMMABLE

I remember when I began to spread like a wildfire

How pyromaniacs salivated and doused gas

on my flames to see how far I could rise.

It was like a match had been lit and my own being was

the combustible material that set me ablaze

I was to blame

And no rain

poured from clouds

to put me out

I was confined to a fire I never wanted to be

I was heat

Burning slowly

BREAKING

Heartbreak hurts

Feelings you can't escape

It's not like broken bones or a scrape

that you know is going to go away

The ache is something you can't get rid of

Only mask, suppress, cover up and pretend is not there

When those emotions resurface

and most often they do

You'll find yourself in tears

Then angry at self

Then at ease

Then at peace

And then back mad again

REGRET

If I could turn back the hands of time

I would interlock my fingers with the short hand and

rotate it in reverse

Age showed me how beautiful

a fairytale it was

to live in a state of bliss

As kids, we used to fear monsters

under our beds

So we slept with our night-lights on

to scare them away

But the monsters have materialized

and as adults

we must now learn to use our inner light

to keep the new monsters away

TIRED

Exhausted.

But

I

Guess

Just

Not

Tired

Enough

To

Leave

TUCKED IN

I feel tucked into silence

Folded like a secret in bedsheet

I don't know truth

Or at least pretend not to

As I wallow in thoughts of uncertainty

Giving no definite yes to my wrongs

I search for wrongs

I found way back when...

I'm rehearsed

Because I've been here before,

Familiar with this low

Predictable,

But too wrapped in my mind

to see everything ain't golden.

Try to shelter myself from woes but find myself one

Coming up short

Been overcompensated

I choose denial

Like the lies I've told

allow comfort

In a body ridden with pain

Where's solitude when you need it?

Does not fortune go with happiness?

Must we choose a piece of grief to accessorize with?

What goes well with a peace of mind?

How flashy will you be?

THE WILLING

God kept sending me signs

But I kept covering my eyes

Because truth be told

I was enjoying being blind

They say ignorance is bliss

But what is it called when you know?

CONSTRUCTION ZONE

I am a construction zone

I warn you

My curves be sharp

and my hills be steep

If you travel my road

I'm sure you'd fall deep

into my debris

and I'll become cemented

in your consciousness

like concrete

I paint lines that stretch

from one end to the next

Me and you together in one lane

Could possibly be a mess,

a head on collision,

or even lead us to a dead end road

But I believe

we got the kind of power

to successfully cross

the kind of bridges

they warn you to avoid when froze

Approach me with caution

Don't move too fast

I do have limits

That I refuse to go pass

To become one together

First, being an ugly mess

is what it may take

Because sometimes you have

to go under construction

to become perfect mates

YOU ARE THE PRIZE!

Do you know how much you are worth? You are valuable and your presence is a gift greater than any amount of money. You must know this and accept nothing less than that. Don't settle!

[Yes, this is a SIGN]

ILLUSION

REPLACEMENT

My side view mirror was shattered.

I didn't anger

Just accepted that it was broken

That the view was distorted and

never to be the same.

Today, I replaced it

with my own hands

and proud to say

I can see clearly now

Today, I learned

that it's okay

to replace things

and people that are shattered

That are distorted

And impair your image

of life and of self.

Because impaired vision

can cause you harm

Can cause you to wreck

And be a wreck!

So replace what you must

if need be

And trust me…

You'll see clearly again

INADEQUATE

I was sorting through my memories,

only to find you left so many dark spots in my mind

And if I were to say something kind,

people might actually believe you were nice.

When truth is, you were colder than ice

And I hate to be the bearer of bad news

but I'm glad the world

No longer has you

It was a joy to see how you left

And if I had had the courage

I would've killed you myself

But instead I settled for metaphors

Metaphorically killed you off

Buried the thoughts of your torment

so deep in a tunnel

that not even God could find it

I planted the insults

you tried to stuff me with

around your tombstone

So that they could grow on you

I left the insecurities you projected

onto me at your gravesite.

So rest in chaos,

In turmoil,

In discomfort,

In suicidal thoughts,

In anxiety,

In depression,

Rest in all the emotions you made me feel

Because now that you are gone

I can finally live

SOUNDS

Love sounds like…

The ring of a phone

the ding of an incoming message

from a lover

It sounds like your fingers furiously colliding

with phone screen

to debunk false allegations of betrayal

It sounds like tirelessly trying to

prove yourself

Love sounds like insecure,

Being degraded and called everything

but beautiful

Like the voicemail he left

hurling insults

Sounds like being called

bitch, slut, and hoe

Being told you'll be replaced

because you don't "follow"

Like the apology he'll give

Like the *unforgiveness* you'll

swallow and

stuff in the back of your throat

and hide behind your eyes

Love sounds like you scraping

around your mind

for positive words to describe yourself

So that you don't

start believing his lies

Love sounds like pleading

to God to help you again

Because love sounds confused

like verbal and mental abuse

From someone who says they love you

PERSONIFY

Love spit in my face

His inability to communicate

made him a haunted house,

a familiar ghost

I tried to convince myself

I wasn't afraid of

I try to run away, but he follows

Trying to force me to participate in an argument

that only he wants to win

I seek refuge in my car

He wants to talk

But I'm only brave enough to

speak through cracked windows

Because his body language is too aggressive

It rattles like a chainsaw.

Too close to my ears

His eyes filled with toxic masculinity

I could tell he wanted to cut me down

to make himself feel tall

Luckily, I was protected

Shielded by the strength

of my doors

But he still found a way

to violate me

Love spit in my face.

Sent the debris of a

double-minded tongue,

laced with particles of hate

Love planted his disgusting saliva

across my face

Love then busted my windows with

his bare hands.

And sadly I'm glad

Just glad it wasn't my eye

like last time

Or my lip

Love spit in my face

And this time I didn't feel nothing

Just acceptance

Maybe denial

Or maybe I was just desensitized

Even still,

I commit myself to the thought

That I am still somebody

I didn't deserve that... because I didn't

And that his poor treatment

is not a reflection of my worth

He is just who he will always be

A conniving monster

Who paints a picture so pretty to the world

that even if I spoke the honest to God truth

about love's abuse

I wouldn't believe me too

SMELLS

Love smells like the blood
dripping from sad eyes
Like a stale breeze.
An aroma similar to salt water lakes
glazing over the cheeks of innocent skin

Smells like ripped fleshed
underneath finger nails
Like sweet poison
clawing at self-esteem

It smells like bleach,
how it destroys
the colors of your happiness

Love smells like toxic waste
Like trash that's supposed to
be another man's treasure
But truth is

that trash will always

be what it is

Therefore, one man's trash

will simply be just another man's trash

It smells like a dump yard of

unresolved conflicts, insults and

bad survival tactics

Like misery scented company

Like the dirt of child trauma

and voids that could never be filled

Love smells so strong

it leaves a stench on

whoever it touches

Love smells like the metal

of sharp knives

held up to protect you against

partners who "love" too hard

Smells like alcohol radiating

From your sorry tongue

Desperately fighting to accept
that this ain't really what love is

Love smells like you coming
into realization that maybe
you don't love yourself

So it then becomes the smell
of a ink on paper
Starts to smell like an escape plan
to self-discovery and self-love

smells like fumes
exhausting from car pipes
Headed far away from
skewed perceptions of love

Because love ain't supposed
to smell like this
like control, belittlement,
like misery, like death,
like a wish to be smothered
and covered in a box of Pinewood

It ain't supposed to smell like smoke

Trying to choke the life out of you

CRAFTY WOLF

They say every dog has its day
but I think every dog has its week.

It's important that you be mindful
of where you decide to sleep.
Word on the street,
Why buy the cow if the milk is free?
Even then, it's still impossible to scope out a fox
when they're all dressed like sheep.

How compatible is the lion and the
lamb? Not likely at all. Often times
in love you don't decide where you
fall.

It's a hard ball to pitch when it
comes to this love game. You got
people who will cry wolf that don't
desire to be saved.

They're just in for the uniform

and recognition they'll

gain.

So be not deceived by the serpent

and his crafty ways

Because not only the weak minded,

but even the strong

get trapped in the bellies of snakes.

WHAT THAT MOUF DO?

When I was in high school

I remember running into one of my classmates

inside the clothing store.

In mid conversation he oddly paused,

painted a smirk on his face,

sunk his 18 year old body into his hips

and fixed his lips to ask me...

"What that mouf do?"

My smile quickly dissolved,

confusion painted my face,

my teenage body folded in uncertainty.

Why was he curious about what my *mouf* do

when he had one too?

So I answered as best as I could...

"Well for starters

This mouth, also known as the Oral Cavity

opens to the outside at the lips.

Its boundaries are defined by
the lips, cheeks, and the hard and soft palate.
It is divided into two sections:
the vestibule, the area between
the cheeks and the teeth, and
the oral cavity proper.
The latter section is mostly filled
by the tongue, which if you didn't
know- is a large muscle that's firmly
anchored to the floor of your mouth
by the frenulum lingual. And in addition
to it's primary role
in the initial digestion of food,
the mouth and its structures are essential
because it assists in the formation of speech.
So if you wondering what this mouth do
it eats and it speaks!"

He slouched in dissatisfaction
and repeated his question with a slightly different
tone "Naw, what that mouth *do*?"

It became obvious that his question
was meant to question my skill level

in performing oral.

It was at 16 that I realized men

don't care about whether or not your mouth can

formulate a cohesive sentence

Or if you use your mouth with intelligence

Some only care if you know how to swallow

them whole and if you can make

your saliva glands produce enough

fluids to satisfy their manhood

But refraining from turning irate

I simply answered…

"This mouth does a multitude of things.

This mouth makes magic happen

It crafts stories to tell

like the one I'm telling now,

to make a point to all girls

that if confronted with such a question,

they make it known

that their mouth do extraordinary things

Like breathe life into hopeless bodies

This mouth speaks life

and can make a difference

This mouth packs a whole lot of power
Because it can have yo' ass
beat for disrespecting me
And in collaboration with my teeth
This mouth chews up the lies you try to feed me,
and process it through my intestine just to shit it out

This mouth screams, complains
It gets loud
This mouth proud!
Something like Harriet Tubman
This mouth gives instructions
Leading enslaved minds to freedom

This mouth form smiles
in the midst of adversity
This mouth Sojourner Truth.
Ain't I a woman?

This mouth do dope shit
Break barriers like Shirley Chisolm
Says "NO" like Claudette Colvin

Who refused to give up her seat

Because this mouth simply

don't bow down to nobody

and it does everything you wish yours could!"

Disappointed again, he replied

"stop with all that deep shit."

YOU ARE ENOUGH

You lack nothing! You are everything and what you offer is enough. Don't get caught up in this world of comparisons, as it is the quickest way to dampen your own spirit. Remember, you are in a race with no one and the only person you need to impress and make proud is you!

OBJECTS OF DESPAIR

NIGHTINGALE

I could tell her wings had been broken

Stolen by love

Her body languished in pain

When she hugged me, I felt

a melancholic energy override my body

Sent a shock of both sympathy and fear

Sympathy... for the pain radiating

from her skin and half smile

Fear... because I saw myself being her

should I continue to make a partner out of poison

I didn't want to end up... her

At a dead end,

Swallowed in regret, what ifs

and should've dones

I noticed how her face shied away

from me, refusing eye contact

How her body slouched with low self esteem

And how her eyes made evident

of what her laugh tried to hide

I imagine she once used to be a strong woman

A free bird with beautiful wings

Why else would she now look down

and not hold her head up proud?

WISDOM

Some people learn the stove is hot by touching it.

The wise learn from seeing others get burned.

MONSTERS

Hey, sis!
I know your introduction to man
Wasn't grand but understand,
all men ain't monsters

They are not all made up of
dust, nails and lose screws
They ain't all waiting
at the back door
of your adolescence
Ready to take
what you don't even know you have yet

They not all waiting to feast
on your self-esteem
Like a thanksgiving meal
That only they can give God thanks for

Some men are the meal

They are Prince Charming

They won't taint your idea of love

They don't come projecting

their trauma on you

And I know your daddy is the root

of your man issues

because of how he abandoned you

But baby girl, lace up your shoes

and get over it or you will continue

making false fathers

out of romantic partners

Don't let his absence make a victim of you

Fix you up to be served like a meal

of low self-esteem to whoever is hungry

You are worth more and you can have better

Listen,

All men ain't monsters

Because some are Prince Charmings

GREEN GRASS

Everybody always talk about the grass

being greener on the other side

But fail to mention

that the darker roots

Are a part of one whole

In front yards

lay patches of dead grass

and browned needles

sprinkled amongst the greener

                                    And more desirable

Somebody should've told you the truth

That NOTHING

is all good

You have to take the bad

with the undesirable

and even if the grass is greener

on the other side

Its darker brothers

Ain't far from it

ATTENDANT

How studious of you to straighten your bed

To make a mess look good

How you stretched your comforter out

and folded the top neatly

But I saw you didn't fix what was underneath.

How you left the bed sheets in disarray

Sometimes we make

problems look pretty

to avoid fixing what's inside

But you can't hide the truth

It will always uncover you

DO THE BAD DIE OLD?

We're all going to die anyway
So what use is being good?
These are words I let coddle
me in comfort and
give me permission to act less
than great after I lost him
When my cousin passed away
I kept hearing people say
"the good die young"
So I made efforts to be bad
to extend my life on this earth

No more Mrs. Nice Guy
I greeted sin with parted lips
and clinched teeth
Because at 13 years old
I lost my 18 year old cousin
and thought it was because
he was simply too good for this earth

But I wish I could pause the moments

leading up to the phone call

we received, informing us he was killed

I'd flow endlessly in that moment

Take my time to breathe

and rewind all our memories

I would pause the last night

he spent with us

when we sat and ate pies

my grandpa made

How we sat in the room and

mocked songs from Jodeci

I'd pause the moment when

we were in elementary and

rode our bikes to school

and struggled our way up the hills

Because even though it was tough

going up, at least we knew our destination

I hate that later on in life I'd find out

how easy it is to fall

To go from being on top

to rolling down a hill

of sadness, anger and regret

I would indefinitely pause

the last time we sat at the table

eating dinner

Pause after the very moment

he made me laugh so hard that

my stomach began to hurt

Because that was the first time

I ever felt that kind of joy

A happiness un-plagued

One that didn't feel guilty

One that was innocent and fun to enjoy

If I could pause right there forever

I'd go to my grave with

untainted memories

Would've left this Earth

not having known pain

And that would've been just fine

BENEFITS

Do your bones not grow tired?
Cry out in desperation for you to stop
stretching them out for people who
wouldn't dare do the same for you?

REWARD

Why do we go through sadness unsure if there's
happiness on the other side?
Why do we act blind, knowing we can see?
Why do we play strong, when in reality we're weak?
Why do we choose love that feels like hate
then blame it on being in a comfortable place?

THEY NEED LOVE TOO

I never liked animals
But always found it cruel
how people imprisoned them in lonely
backyards and cages with only enough
room to lay in one spot

I always found it weird
how depriving them of being
around their own kind
could make one feel happy

Imagine being like them...
Used as an accessory
of companionship
To only be summoned
for affection on days that feel
too empty to swallow

See, I know why caged things sing

They sing like a person in a one-sided relationship

They sing because they're lonely

Expected to be the carriers of weight

and the givers of comfort and happiness

The caged ones sings

Because it lives in fear

In fear of disappointing

the ones who use them solely

for their benefit,

Never to be reciprocated

It fears not having a purpose,

Not being needed

Hell, it fears not being used

Because that's what it's become accustomed to

The caged one sings because

It's the only thing that tunes out

the truth

The truth that they are not truly loved

Just objects of validations

for subjective lovers

Just placeholders

for when things fall apart

The caged one sings because

it don't know no other way

to cope with his pain

PUT THE WORK IN UNTIL IT WORKS OUT

Believing is one of the most powerful gifts you can feed your mind. There's power in your thoughts and in what you speak. Anything you want in this life you can have it as long as you believe it and put in the work to obtain it. So believe in yourself because all great accomplishments begin with a mere thought. Tell yourself you are beautiful, you are enough, you will achieve your dreams, you will attract and maintain healthy relationships and that you are deserving of the best that life has to offer. Never stop working on your dreams.

BROKEN
PEACE

STUCK...

Feels like being disconnected from self,

from friend, from family

Feels like wishing to be the past

Hoping for a better future

Feels like frustration,

an unstable tongue,

a tightness in your chest.

Like choking back rivers,

a tall death,

resentment in breath.

Not wanting to acknowledge

being weak

Feels like too much,

not enough,

a fountain of conflict

Being forced into war

Feels like turmoil,

a constant wonder

Like a wish to go back to normal

POST TRAUMATIC RELATIONSHIP DISORDER

The woman is NOT the victim in this ONE!

Because this time
She was the one with the dagger
Shooting innocent men down
Force feeding them lies
with nice silverware

SHE was the cheater
The one who didn't realize what she had
until it was gone
This time she was in the wrong
The one having to
Callll Tyroneeee
to help her get her shit
Y'all she wasn't shit

And definitely NOT a victim

Because the woman is not a victim in this one

Because she not suffering from a heart break

Or crying about how a nig--

I mean a boy… did her wrong

In this one right here,

the woman is the victor.

Operating on the winning side

She not the one crying in this story

Because this time she got the long

end of the stick

See instead,

this is an attempted coming of age story

about a girl who never learns to grow up

or accept accountability for her toxic behaviors

Who never understood loyalty

And took much pleasure in leading men on

Just to drop them off

in places where they would forever be stained.

She has no shame in being a *manizer* and blaming

everybody else for why she can't keep it real

The man is the victim is this one

He's the one who's having to question his self-worth

The one who's confused about how he gave his all just

to be used and discarded like day old news

The man is the one sobbing and crying

Praying and asking God to lift that pain out his body

He'll be the one with

PTSD

PTRD... Post Traumatic Relationship Disorder

The one who'll have flashbacks of the

betrayal he suffered at the hands of the

one who said they loved him

He'll wake up from nightmares of his lover

cheating on him, just to find out it was all true

He'll be the one regretting saying I do.

The one obsessing daily about the status of their

relationship

Wondering if it'll work out,

if they will survive the bad days

He'll be the one that's paranoid

Because the man is the victim in this one

and not the lady

I'm tired of hearing stories of the lady

who was treated bad at the hands of a man

The one who was used and abused

Naw!

the woman the victor in my story

She full of joy and high self-esteem

She ain't looking to fill voids her daddy planted in her

She's a beautiful seed, a rose straight out of concrete

She no longer looking up to the older

folks as relationship goals because truth be told

big Mama only stayed with Pawpaw

because he paid the bills

But they say when you know better you do better.

And the women in her family taught her

not to be weak and too dependent

She's the one with the *big egooooo!*

She'll drop a dude like a bad habit

and won't think twice about it

Because she know there's plenty fish in the sea to see

And she got enough love to spread.

She not pretending to be no magician

like other women

Who think they can fix a man

Who enjoys being broken

Abra cadabra poof!

Disrespect her once and she'll go ghost on you

Because the lady not the victim in this story

That storyline far too played out

SOMEBODY'S DAUGHTER

No lie

My Mama taught me how

to do paperwork in elementary

I knew social security numbers,

addresses and phone numbers

by heart

My memory was impeccable

Even memorized the stroke of

her signature

Though my handwriting was

underdeveloped I still

signed her name on documents

whenever need be

In 9th grade

I took that skill

and I signed myself up for baseball

at the community center

In all honesty

I only joined for the uniform because
I wanted to feel a part of something

But I never imagined doing something
that was supposed to be fun
would be a figment of an unjust memory
consistently reminding me of who
I am not and will never be

I watched dads celebrate their
mediocre children from the stands
while mine was nowhere to be found

It's strange how all it took was one summer
to drag my self-esteem and feelings
of inadequacy across 10 years
of trying to overcompensate

But I remember my Mama taught me
how to be self-sufficient,
how to get myself through,
how to memorize things that matter
How to step in for yourself

So I imagined myself my own Dad

When I played on the field

I looked to myself and celebrated me

Not worrying about my father deficiency

Because I'm too old and it's too late

I will never be a man's daughter

Though I wish I was and could've been

EGGSHELLS

Tiptoeing around insecurities

Trying to find subjects to walk on that don't creak

Like an outcry of desperation

Walking around sunken spaces

Sure not to put pressure

In places that had already been made fragile

Speaking in kind tones,

side eyeing,

waiting for the moment

it all falls down

Because it always do

Stretching out the inevitable

Like you don't know you've

come to the end of the road

But fear made a friend out of loneliness

Then made a residence in your temple

Because strength don't know you yet

Self-esteem don't know you yet

Faith don't know you yet

You don't know you yet

WAYS

Though I was ready to part ways

I secretly wanted him to beg

To satisfy this feeling of inadequacy inside me

I wished he would beg

So I could feel the power

I let him steal from me

I wanted to feel like he actually cared

When I know he didn't

I wanted him to beg because

I thought it would validate me

Paint me the belief that I was desired and valued

I wanted him to beg

To make leaving easy

So when I denied his plea

I would feel like I had the upper hand

I wanted him to beg

To feel ashamed of himself for what he did

I wanted him to learn a lesson

Realize I was a blessing

Moreso,

I wanted to do him

how he did me.

GASLIGHT

He told me I wasn't enough

That he loved me

But preferred me paired

With another woman to satisfy his ego

And I've always felt inadequate

So when he told me he needed

More than what I could provide

I couldn't help but cry

Why?

Would he say that to me

Knowing I struggled

with being enough all my life

Like how I used to fight hard

to go above and beyond

so that the man who told his wife my name was

"whatsaname" would find me interesting enough to

claim as his own child

Wow!

Did this asshole really just say that to me?

He must not have a heart

No respect or regard

for my feelings

What was he thinking?

I got so mad

that I wanted to say some mean shit

Like...

Fuck you bitch!

You hoe!

You should've left me alone!

That's why yo' teeth short

And not proportionate with yo' face

I wanted to know how belittlement would taste

falling off the tip of my tongue

and planting itself on his self-esteem

So that he felt just like me

Trapped beneath

the wings of extreme inadequacies

But the thing about how people interpret situations

Is that our perception of it

is only powered by a collection of feelings we have
toward ourselves
So when he told me he wanted other women
I concluded it was because I wasn't enough but that
was only because that's what I felt about myself.
And I was only projecting it on to him so that I didn't
have to be responsible for my own baggage

Not enough?
Such a recurring theme in my life
But in light
of that epiphany
I realized he wasn't telling me that I wasn't enough
He was actually trying to tell me that he was sick
And I was so wrapped up in my thoughts
I missed it.

GASLIGHT PART II

Sick?

He had an eating disorder

A binge eating disorder!

Which is

"The act of compulsive overeating —

That in return produces

Emotional, psychological and

physiological side effects

that can dramatically compromise

one's quality of life and hope for the future"

He was compromising

our hope for the future

Because he didn't know

how to stop consuming

beyond a full belly

He had a problem

With over indulging in women

Like even though he was full

He wanted to keep eating

Sinking his teeth deep in white,

black and yellow meat

Sacrificing his health, he didn't think

Over and over like a record on repeat

No Charlie Brown

But he often had me like "goOod grief"

Addicted to busting and

consuming pecans and peanuts

With Lucy, Peppermint Patty,

Frieda, Violet and Marcie

Even tried to suggest polygamy

in attempt to remedy

The issue of his disloyalty

He was fascinated about trying

To see how much his belly could hold

Not realizing how damaging

His actions would be

Emotionally…

He was tearing us apart

Causing a distance

Because of how much he lied

to disguise his addiction

Psychologically...

His desires started interfering

with my self-worth

and making his diminish

Physiologically...

He started to look old

Because they say too much sex ages you

However, I refuse to let his sickness

Impede on my happiness

Let his bad habits destroy my self-esteem

Or let his shortcomings short change me

Or let his darkness dim my light

Or let his insecurities make a residence

out of my temple

I refuse to believe that

I have to suffer to feel love

Or that I have to endure mistreatment

Because "a man is going to be a man"

Not bending over backwards

to accommodate him while

minimizing myself to make him feel

like the man he never was

And probably never will be

Won't let nobody convince me

to follow and be submissive to a lost cause

Because how can a man be willfully blind

then expect a woman to trail behind?

SAVE YOURSELF

If you are waiting for someone to help you or save you... you are wasting your time. You must figure out a way to uplift yourself and execute on your goals when nobody's there to support. You have to pick yourself up when you're feeling low. You have to be your own superhero and never make excuses for why you are not where you want to be emotionally, physically, or financially.

FRAMES

PLUS SIZE THIGHS

To my ladies with legs they have to shop in separate

sections for

Large hips, big arms and calf muscles

That only fit in the wide sized knee-high boots

To my large, extra-large, 1x and up

My girls with thighs that cause so much friction

when they walk they rub holes in their jeans

Your thick thighs been saving lives

since before time

Swallowing heads and bearing babies

You are more than beautiful

Don't live in your body

Trying to please everybody else

Let them know

You don't pick out outfits for nobody's approval

Your body isn't good at hide and seek

And that beauty is not synonymous

with small, skinny and slim

Beauty come in big sizes too

So to my big girls

with big bodies

You got nothing to be ashamed of

Don't you hide your fat like stain on a white T-shirt

Be proud

And never walk with your head down

WOMAN EXPERIENCE

I don't like being a lady

I wish I were born butterfly or bird

No, I wish I would stop wishing

I were things I am not

But I don't like being woman

Since birth we're taught to be scared

to beware of predators

Because for some reason it must be harder

to teach men how to keep their hands to themselves

To not enter places they weren't invited to

that a woman's clothing is not an

invitation for sexual harassment

I hate that I'm thought of as fragile and weak

I hate how calculated I have to be

in my response to cat calls like…

"Aye, you with the thick legs, let me talk to you"

And to tell the truth

If I weren't afraid that he'd curse me out

I'd tell him that his teeth were so yellow,

that I knew if he didn't care about himself

He had no room to care about me

But instead I choose to respond kindly

"Thank you, but no thank you"

I hate that I feel scared when I walk from

my car to my apartment door at night

Like the distance between my Toyota Camry

and front porch feels like a death walk

I hate I was trained to be weak

To be soft

To play with Barbie Dolls

To be too forgiving and too tolerating

If "woman" was a painting, it'd be a doormat

Because some seem to think we're a place they can

wipe their dirt off to make themselves clean

Why women got a niche for nurturing dead things

 like dead men and relationships

at dead ends

Was that supposed to be a gift or a curse?

I hate that our worth

is measured by the amounts of pain we can take

I hate how tedious the task be to care for a vagina,

how inconvenient having breasts are,

how they get in the way when you sleep or workout

I never asked to be female

a woman laced with lady parts

This was not my choice

But I have learned to live with it

Afterall, nobody likes a girl who frowns

And after being told so many times

I should remember to smile by now

Like I wear this face for your amusement

Like my emotions should be tucked away

between pursed lips and clenched teeth

And contrary to male belief I am not an object

You cannot control me

I am a human with thoughts, opinions and feelings

I am not to be fucked with because even in my despair

being a woman has its beauty,

more glory and advantage

So on a positive note…

What I do love about being a woman is that I have the

power to carry life in my womb.

To reproduce whole human beings

and nurture them with nourishment

from my own body

I can lose blood and still live

I have so much to give

Though I get mad when you take

and never give back

I don't hold grudges

Because the love in me

is bigger than you'll ever be worthy of

I love being a woman because…

Beyoncé is a woman,

Oprah Winfrey is a woman,

Michelle Obama is a woman.

So ain't it clear how powerful we are

Backbones who provide stability to unstable things

So I love being a woman and I don't wish to be

anything other than what I already am

A woman.

WIPER BLADES

And then my hands

turned into wiper blades

Pushing back oceans of failure

Now ready to see

There's no trail of mishap

that could ever blind me

DESPISE

I despise,

all the lies

I've been told

So in the palm of my hand

is the grudge I hold

WEIGHT

You need to lose some weight

You getting big and you can't hide it

Girl, you heavy

And you can't hurry up

Because you got too much stuff

You've been dragging

I bet I could measure your grief in pounds

I can tell them burdens been weighing you down

You have to let some of those bags go

Nobody asked you to carry the world,

Nobody put you in charge of

managing misfortunes or made you

Captain "Solve Everybody Problems"

You did this to yourself

It's time you let go, allow yourself to grow

And stop worrying about other folks

SELF-DOUBT

I went to his funeral today

I almost felt guilty for not feeling sad

But it was satisfying to see him lowered in the ground

PERIOD

My Mama had to know

I'd grow up

to write poems

to like words

And would take them all too personal

So she filled me with affirmations

that I would need,

to feed and clothe my self-esteem

She knew I would become a noun

A person,

Sometimes a place,

Sometimes a thing

Depending on whose hands

I'd fall in and out of

But I'm sure my Mama would tell me

"Don't you ever second guess

your worth.

You are the complete sentence

Not to be treated like a fragment

or incomplete thought

You are full of adjectives.

Words to describe you are-

talented, smart, and beautiful

You are an action word

A verb

I birthed you solution based

Made you to teach and reach

You will be powerful when you speak

You are the prize

An exclamation in my eyes

So don't believe

the enemies' lies when you hear it

Because you are fearless

and wonderfully made"

Period.

YOU SHOULD SMILE

I

am

not

obligated

to

pretend

for

you.

STOP LYING

Stop lying to yourself about who you are. If you can honestly identify the things you struggle with, you can then actively work to become better. Be honest, do you really give your full effort toward your goals whether it be business, fitness or relationships? If not, take a moment to see how you can be intentional in improving yourself then do it!

GLASS
SHARDS

BAD BUSINESS

He was here for business

I was here for love

That's why we never on the same accord

DE-GARDENED

Once a flower has been uprooted

Only for the pleasure of eyes

Stripped from its

roots and disconnected

from its lifeline

It will not grow

Remember,

no matter how much water

you offer a rose

after it's been picked

it will die

DIY

When it's time to be happy

When it's time to execute,

When it's time to win,

When it's time to heal,

When it's time to rise up,

When it's time to get it done,

When it's time to be relieved,

When it's time to succeed

DO. IT. YOURSELF!

SCREENSHOTS

Even if the memories grow faint and fade

The truth still remains

the same and unchanged

SUBMISSIVE

I got no more arm and leg to give

No more length in my back to bend over backwards

No more care to trace around your ego

All out of understanding and soft words

No more chill.

Frozen over like ice cubes

Until someone find me of use

Decide to place me in cup

of water

of juice

or alcohol

Depending of what you choose

Determines how bad or good I am for you

I may nourish you,

or be too sweet to be any

good for your health

Or I may alter your state of being

So what beverage will you bring to the table?

I can only give what you put out

Therefore, if you find this thing to be good,

unhealthy or toxic

It'll all be a reflection of you.

STAGE ACCEPTANCE

There's a hate brewing in my heart

a disconnect,

an end I anticipate

to be ridden tragic

but so sweet,

I gather it a burden to be this happy

and sad at the same time.

But I won't let pain touch my tongue

 I won't weep

Won't let defeat seep through my teeth

ENDING

I know what I feel

I'm not confused

Or misconstrued

Just in disbelief

A state of denial

Not wanting the truth

Even when I had the proof

Ignoring the facts

Sensing deceit in the

way that he acts

Energy is off

His voice is tough

He criticizes me

And complains about stupid stuff

I can feel the turn

The coldness in his eyes

I hate that moments with him

No longer make time fly

Feeling on edge

Scared to breathe or talk

I can tell it's over

Defeat written all over his walk

LIFE IS ABOUT PERSPECTIVE

Life is full of up and downs. No one is exempt from hardships. It's guaranteed that you will experience some kind of grief in your life. But guess what? YOU get to choose how you will let it affect you! There's many ways to cope with these pains. Some people turn to drugs, sex, and or engulf themselves in work to deal with their burdens. But one thing is for certain, it is YOU who has the power to decide if you will let the negative things in your life make or break you. Choose wisely.

REFLECT

NO MISTAKES

You weren't put on earth by mistake

Start accepting accountability

for the decisions you make

And role you play

in your own demise.

Don't be nobody's victim

You are a winner

Even if sometimes you lose

SOLUTION BASED

I was waiting for someone to help me

Then I thought

"why don't you help YOURSELF?"

PERSPECTIVE

Life is about perspective

So when shit happens

... because it will

YOU have to choose

how you will let it affect you

LIVING

Being able to speak

Without fear of my own truth

hurting somebody else

DUST YOURSELF OFF

Don't worry when you fall

You get to get back up

And try again

NOT WORRIED

And I'll go to my grave with a smile

Unworried about what I could not change

And thankful for what all I did

LIFE CAN BE...

Life can be
a traumatizing experience
But you live with it
Learn that trauma is something
everybody wears
You are not the only one
Though you feel alone

Some people just find nice things
to accessorize their pain with
Like nice clothes,
money,
the infamous smile,
the "yeah I'm okay"
We learn to cover the familiar
To give it a unique face so
that it ain't easily recognizable

We trick ourselves into believing we are okay

Until it's no longer feasible to pretend

Until that smile can't fit over that sad face and frown

Until our mouths can't muster up the courage to

force our lips to say shit it don't really mean

because truth is

We   ain't   okay.

KEEP GOING

It is always easy to abort mission

To quit before the finish

To be able to say you stopped

before finding out

if you could survive the ending

> Don't let yourself die in wars
> you could very well win

CHOOSING

If someone shows you who they are…

Believe them

Because the truth can't lie when

it's not on tongue

It has motion and moves in certain ways

It sways

Believe love for what it does

And not for what it say

Don't let nobody use you

Make you a victim

You were born to be a victor

And one day you'll realize the bondage

you in, was caused by the chains

you put on your own two feet

Stop acting blind,

when you got the key

to your own relief

Free from deceit and false beliefs

How will you choose to live?

Because you don't have to be victimized no more,

You don't have to compromise no more,

You don't have to sympathize no more

You just have to choose to live

COMPLIMENTS

Sis, you are a walking piece of art!

Look at that jaw bone

How those ears go

perfect with your shape.

You could be a model

You popping!

You glowing!

Sis, who raised you?

I love your hair

Look at how colors compliments your skin

You are so beautiful

I mean look at your elbows

And the structure of your nose

You remind me of a rose.

You so pretty

You look like you are at peace

Your voice strong when you speak

You are so talented

and worthy… don't you ever doubt it!

What does your reflection say about you?

15 out of the 17 mirrors in my first apartment

"If well used, however, the mirror can aid moral meditation between man and himself. Socrates urged young people to look at themselves in mirrors so that, if they were beautiful, they would become worthy of their beauty, and if they were ugly, they would know how to hide their disgrace through learning. The mirror, a tool by which to **"know thyself,"** invited man to *not* mistake himself for God, to avoid pride by knowing his limits, and to improve himself. His was thus not a passive mirror of imitation but an active mirror of transformation."

-Diogenes

MESSAGE FROM THE AUTHOR

UN-FUCK YOURSELF

We stand in our own way. Often times we are so afraid to leave the familiar behind in order to create a better and new reality. We hold on to shitty jobs, relationships and ways of thinking because we fear the unknown. We fuck ourselves out of opportunities and happiness when we choose to settle. So un-fuck yourself today and live the life you deserve!

ABOUT DREKKIA WRITES

Drekkia is a 25 year old spoken word artist. She is a first generation college student who graduated from the University of Central Arkansas with her Bachelors of Business Administration in Insurance and Risk Management.

She has always been naturally talented in writing. In elementary she won numerous creative writing awards. In high school she started the first poetry club at eStem

Charter High School and organized serval events for artists. She was voted Most Talented, Fall Queen, Miss eStem, and Most Likely to be Famous by her peers. At 18 she joined the Foreign Tongues Poetry Troupe as the youngest member and began traveling the states doing poetry.

Morning started the organization BARE Arts on the UCA college campus, which was designed to provide a consistent platform for performing and visual artists to showcase their talent and to teach them how to make a living doing what they love.

During her time at UCA, she created and hosted a weekly radio show known as the BARE Arts Radio Show (B.A.R.S) that showcased local artists every Thursday.

Drekkia also spearheaded one of the most popular sex education programs called Sex on Stage. This event uses performing arts to promote sex health, discuss common sex myths, and to encourage students to get tested in support of the UCA Health Center's Get Yourself Tested "GYT" campaign.

She is as a Creative Career Coach, Behavior Coach, Teaching Artist, Spoken Word Artist, Motivational Speaker and Author. As a coach, she teaches creatives how business and art commingle. As a teaching artist, for the past 5 years she has taught the art of poetry and creative writing to at-risk youth to help improve their communication, comprehension and coping skills. Drekkia also worked as a Behavior Coach in an alternative-to-suspension program where she used her art to teach behavior modification to troubled students.

In all, Drekkia is an agent of change and lover of words and people.

Join my online community on Facebook

1. hey, sis!

A girl group designed to unite women through networking events, photoshoots, and hangouts. We gather to celebrate the beauty and intelligence of all women.

2. Write More!

A community of writers who share original poetry and creative writing. We gather for weekly writing challenges and help each other strengthen our skills as writers.

Website: www.drekkia.com

Instagram: @Drekkia

Twitter: DrekkiaWrites

SnapChat: @Drekkia

Facebook: Drekkia Writes

Email: DrekkiaWrites@gmail.com

Love you

Bye! ☺

66664059R00080

Made in the USA
Columbia, SC
19 July 2019